"we create
create wonders."
Chandan Sharma

COLUMBUS
CREATIVE
COOPERATIVE

~~Dearest~~ Rollie & Marilyn
we hope you will enjoy
this body of work. we found
it in a local shop and thought
of you both. Please enjoy!
all our love,
Joshua &
Taylor

OTHER BOOKS BY
COLUMBUS CREATIVE COOPERATIVE

The Ides of March
An Anthology of Ohio Poets

Edited By
Hannah Stephenson

Proudly Presented By

COLUMBUS CREATIVE COOPERATIVE

WWW.COLUMBUSCOOP.ORG

Pauquette ltd
dba Columbus Creative Cooperative
P.O. Box 91028
Columbus, OH 43209
www.ColumbusCoop.org

CONTENT EDITOR
Hannah Stephenson

PRODUCTION EDITOR
Brad Pauquette

Cover artwork by Yao Cheng
Design by Brad Pauquette

Print ISBN 978-0-9890645-0-7
Ebook ISBN 978-0-9890645-1-4

Printed in the United States of America
1 3 5 7 9 10 8 6 4 2

Contents

Introduction

This anthology is a call to embrace the Ides of March. No need to beware while reading work from these Ohio poets.

When I moved back to Columbus (my hometown) from the West Coast a few years ago, I was immediately struck by the wealth of literary talent here. As a poet, I was especially delighted to meet and discover my fellow poet-Ohioans (Poehioans?).

Working with Columbus Creative Cooperative on this anthology of poems has reassured me, overwhelmingly, that the voices of Central Ohio poets are plentiful, strong, and richly varied.

Our approach to the Ides of March theme has been flexible and open. The poems in this collection explore diverse facets of the concept; they touch on ideas of spring and the month of March, middles and centers, in-betweenness, senators, power, revolution and conspiracy, fortune-tellers, cautionary tales, ambition, sharp knives, and much more.

I'm so proud to present you with the poems you are about to enjoy. Lend me your ears (and eyes), and I promise to return them to you more beguiled, rejuvenated, and inspired.

Lions and lambs,
Hannah Stephenson

1

Everyone's Sky

Steve Abbott

Morning is often like this, full of prayers
for the green spot of a traffic signal
announcing smooth movement in rush hour,
small gift in a universe spinning
obstacles from their own orbits into

my groundless expectations, unquestioned
assumptions about how each day unfolds as if
designed in some celestial draftsman's software.
Near the corner of Summit and 7th,
an old woman and a girl in red boots

move through the monochrome sleet,
where their diluted, soundless shapes
offer counterpoint to the world's
daily breakfast of disaster pouring
starvation, earthquake and murder

from the radio as if the grey dome
of winter is everyone's sky and nothing
beneath it will ever be dry or warm again,
no one to tell me otherwise.
At work we complain about the president

and talk about the earthquake.
We sip coffee, mumble pity and destiny,
question or curse the divine plan, maybe
wonder at the depth of its mystery.
I never mention the red boots.

Evidence

Steve Abbott

On her morning walk, the dog takes her
from one sniff-spot to the next.
There is no other path.
Overnight, snow, and already the way
is marked with evidence of other dogs,
boots, an overlay of treads and paws.
She's been gone an hour, and I'm on
my second cup of coffee, steam rising
from the chimneys down Findley Avenue
beyond the backyard's pale blue frieze.
The snow has deepened, there is
no other path than what has transformed
the narrow brick walk into a line
of drift, the way only a hint of shadow.

She'll be back soon, making tea, sharing
news of who she talked to in the park,
Indianola's plowed-in sidewalks,
the house on Calumet sold at last.
She plans to do some laundry, finish her book.

This is the path. Overnight, snow.
In the yard, a stray dog's footprints.

I Begin To Understand the Video Age

Steve Abbott

Persian Gulf War, 1991

By 11 p.m., four hours after the bombing
of Baghdad began, a ceremonial drumbeat
marched a promotional ad across the ABC screen,
where through an ooze-green lens I took part
in night-scope bomb runs and the skyline pulsed
blue below anti-aircraft tracers arcing
phosphorous stars toward home, like a Christmas card
slashed with golden arches as video clips
I'd been buried by earlier that evening
sparked behind the sturdy Times typeface
The Gulf War
that spun up over computer graphics of tanks
and fighter jets, radar locking on symbols
of something pumping coolly distant through
my intact veins while a serious voice cautioned me to
Stay with ABC and I began to follow orders,
the fastest TV promotion ever bringing me war
Live! as satellites merged White House flacks
with white bursts of flak above Baghdad
and its Al Rashid Hotel, where an American reporter
spoke from the darkened rooftop to my living

room as I watched a decade of high-tech progress
in munitions being field-tested against targets
they were designed for, invisible people beneath
collapsed walls and words and reports
and reporters, continuous percussion of updates
flashing out of recent memory to link with
the soundtrack's kettle drums beating the air
from within me, breath suspended like a flare
in the downlink of destruction, lungs collapsing
smothered in concussion and visual bombardment
syncopated to the chorus of my own marching feet.

What She Brought

MJ Abell

3 mallard eggs nestled in Tupperware,
dull taupe as if to stay hidden in the pine
needles where she found them. Each smaller
than a chicken egg, heavy with hopeless
unborn life. Cold now, abandoned
when the shifts of this tempestuous spring
drove mothers away from their nests,
too confused to weather it out.

1 Canada goose egg, creamy offwhite,
filling my whole palm with fragile silence.
The clinging bits of brown –
are they from the mother's body,
what the nurses wipe off, the slime
I was surprised to love in its slippery
necessity, its beginningness.

I thank her for the eggs
and at last forgive her, my mother
whose basket must carry
the tenderness I always wanted
somewhere, that day swaddled
in tissue, saved for her journey to us,
to show my children –
to show me, her egg,
the one that was born,
that split the shell of her.

The Day My Grandfather Died

Nin Andrews

You will know when someone you love is dying, my father always said. *You don't need a prophet or a soothsayer or a bird to fly in your window. Sometimes the dead even drop by to say goodbye, even if they live miles away. And I don't mean in person. Not exactly.*

Nonsense, my mother said.

Well, that's what happened when my father died.

It didn't. You never even tell that story the same way twice, my mother said.

It did. It happened in July, the year of 1939 when there hadn't been a drop of rain since late April, a year when a hot wind blew into town during the dogwood festival and coated the town in white petals. If you had been riding in a plane and just happened to look down, you might have thought there was snow on the ground, but pretty soon all the petals turned to brown and smelled like rotten apricots.

I've never smelled a rotten apricot in my life.

You have. You smell it every spring during dogwood season. Like rotten eggs and fruit, all mixed up together.

Dogwoods don't smell.

They do. And they sure did that year. Everything smelled rotten that year. And everything went wrong. The chickens stopped laying, the cows' milk soured before it reached the table, and the corn barely came out of the ground before the earworms and the Japanese beetles moved in, and all their tassels turned to slime. It was a year the folks around town called a good year to die since no one was having any fun being alive. In fact the local paper had to hire an extra staff member just to cover the obituaries.

They didn't have to hire anyone new, my mother said.

They did. They hired Jerry Combs. From Memphis, Tennessee that June.

Because he needed a job, my mother said, *and his father worked at The Daily Progress.*

His father said it was because more folks were dying than ever before.

I am sure he did say that.

By mid-July, my father said, *it was so hot, no one could sleep at night, and no one could stay awake during the day. Even the flies stopped buzzing. The few that took flight, fell out of the sky and rolled over on their backs, kicking their little fly legs in the air. It was so hot the crickets started a fire in Joe Milton's alfalfa field, just by rubbing their wings together. You could hear the sirens screaming for hours, the black plumes of smoke filling the horizon. It was so hot that when you went down to the garden to water the vegetables in the morning, the tomatoes burst open at the seams. You didn't have to cook them for breakfast. They were already fried.*

I never ate a fried tomato fresh out of the garden, my mother said.

You don't like fried tomatoes, so of course you didn't eat one. That year they were hot tomatoes right off the vine. You just had to stir them into the grits.

I don't like tomatoes in my grits.

You don't know what you're missing, my father continued. *Maybe it was the heat, and maybe it was a migraine coming on strong that day in July, the 15th, 1939, but when I looked out across the cow pasture, I saw my father walking toward me even though he was dying in his bed down in Raleigh, North Carolina. He was wearing a white suit. And when my father saw me that last time, he started waving, first with his hands, then his arms, then his whole body, waving and waving. The next thing I saw he was rising into the sky. He looked like a white handkerchief, growing smaller and smaller. Then he was like a piece of unlined paper, tossed in the wind, and then he was just a fleck of wandering ash. Then he was gone. I turned to Jane when I stepped inside. That was my father, come to say goodbye, I said. Who? she asked. What are you talking about? I said to her that my father has just passed. I took out my hanky and began to cry.*

If

Nin Andrews

_____

If you spill salt, toss a pinch
right hand over left shoulder
or bad luck will happen
to the one you love.

If you pass a graveyard,
hurry
before the dead steal a strand of your hair.
In this way, many have gone bald.

If you fall asleep asking a question,
you will wake with the answers
God has given.
He will take them back
if you don't write them before 10 AM.

If you think of someone 3 times
in one day,
their soul is calling your name.

If you tell a lie,
you will look down and to the left
and your nose will drip.

If you wake before 7 AM on the first day
of the month, say *bunny, bunny*
and good luck will follow
for seven days.

If a bird flies into the house,
the angels will visit soon.

If you see a ghost on the beach,
leave immediately,
or your house will be washed to sea.

If you listen to your heart beat
very carefully,
the distance between one beat
and the next will lengthen.
In this way
you can live as long as you please.

Two Kinds of Folk

Nin Andrews

There are two kinds of folks in this world, my father always said. *Those who believe in magic, and those who don't. Sometimes you aren't sure which you are. You might find out when you least expect it.* He said it happened to him during World War Two.

How, he could never explain exactly. Only that he was on leave from the military in Portland, Oregon, and suddenly he was driving into Seattle, Washington. He remembered glancing down to tune the radio, thinking he needed some classical tunes to soothe his nerves, maybe some Mozart or Chopin, and when he looked up again, the road looked different. And Mount Rainier leaned up against the sky. It was all so clear, so sudden, the revelation of who-knows-what-happened cut him like a knife. He felt as if he were held in an envelope of light, even as his car raced him outside of time and place and his last iota of common sense. He kept driving and driving, feeling the wind on his face, thinking about the distance between what is real and what a man thinks or believes. After that, he started noticing things he'd never seen. Like the lace on the wings of dragonflies that floated above the river outside his place, like the sound of his own heartbeat keeping him awake late into the night. Like the memory of 4:00 in the afternoon on July 8, 1942, the day he saw his buddy, Joe, take his last breath. Every night he still said *goodnight, Joey,* before he closed his eyes. He could have sworn Joey was near, listening and waiting for one last dream.

Spring Buds

David Baker

His might bloom, as a green thing will, or wilt
with weather or the market's temperament.
He's your trader, he's your brother, or not
your brother if you're nodding there slouched
on a cardboard flat beside the bookstore.
Food, or coke, or weed in that case, or sex,
as his is the green roughage of money.

And hers, who keeps pace with him, power-blue
suit, Hermes silk, gym shoes, orating air,
is likely money, too. And hers—"Buddy,
this girl gets up early [pause] for *no man* . . ."
—is renegotiating family ties.
As all along the walk heads are bobbing,
ears planted with their tiny buds, one, two

per head sometimes, row on row of fertile
dreaming (hers, lunch—his, who knows—his, dancing
a funky two-step in a hat, says, grinning,
"exercise"). As what may grow is a field
of hopes, given water, given sun: this
cold city set to dreaming, given time,
given money, or just a hint of song.

This poem first appeared in The Yale Review
and is reprinted with permission of the poet.

March

Joshua Butts

For L.A.M. and Purdue Pharma (producers of OxyContin)
It's hard to carry
a television, even a small television
given the guts and back story
where the swindling really happens,
where other humans and actor dogs and actor ghouls
and actor country singers
appear thrown through wires.
But ____, you carry the TV
down the street anyway—
the heavy black box to your heavy place.
Family knows they have to call first.
You could become widely known
and just might if caught walking
with the five o'clock news
down the street just a few minutes early.
This poem isn't hard to write
because I trust that you will live,
that we all will live.
Salem cemetery is filling up
more or less in the right order.
But when you carry the television

be sure to think about your lower back.
Someday your kitchen floor
or basket of laundered clothes
will need you to be strong—ready
for the basics. But I know it
is hard—I am not joking—
and I know that you are not a crazy person
carrying a television
though you are carrying a television.
May all our souls be pure and then
we can judge. But souls are never pure
and the bright blows of morning sunlight
and the hallows of night kill
any sense of purity—the Easter grass,
the coronation of a perfect life—
but somehow, there's always wire
for the television.

A Hand Reaches Out from the Dull Gray Sky in March

Joshua Butts

I don't want a name.
But I shake the hand,
hoping it will go.

I can't tell if the gray
is from buildings
or the countryside.

Fevers never come
from the sky but
from the heat of the earth

like a sunburn's heat comes
from auburn skin,
or strawberry skin.

No one is uncomfortable in hell
for constantly they think,
I'll get used to this.

But if there were a counterpoint
cool—would it be so alluring
to not need heat?

They Can Start Swimming in March

Joshua Butts

is a line in a song I wrote in the
winter of '05 on a weighted-key

synthesizer as the furnace was muted
and the glowing lights and microphones

appeared like sharp points in a room
warmed by the quiet furnace

where in spite of the heat
the winter snow filled up the stairs.

In other seasons players pulled up to help,
to stay for a few days.

Just before breakfast a tambourine
would appear on your plate.

You could either shake it or move it away
for the cantaloupe. The rooms were made

of walls but we painted them.
Our parents either loved the colors

or hated the colors but the conversation
was always about the neighbors.

In the new place the couple speaks
through the wall. We can hear as he arrives

for an evening visit with his silent dog.
He whistles to let Raven (her dog) know of friendly arrival.

They are a couple that just hang out. They
laugh oddly. I think of how one must've taught

the other how to laugh in the short
days and months. I think of the old place.

It's already March. There are no bugs here,
but they are about to hatch. Everyone is sneezing—

the sneeze is jumping into the wires
and moving and telling all about the sneeze.

The neighbor has been hunting feathers.
I heard her tell him last night: "Jack, it wasn't easy."

The History Channel Seeks Answers in Outer Space

Nikkita Cohoon

We are all done for:
Ask the Mayans—
see what's been left
behind, decoded.
Nostradamus provides an excuse

to hold hands tighter—
I've endured any number of abductions.

My descriptions and drawings no different from any
Other—

They wear skinny jeans if they are dressed at all, snuffing
whole galaxies through teardrop nostrils their eyes sink
in the ocean, create pockmarks blacker than those murky
bottoms. Their mouths are the worst, indifferent gashes
uttering over and over *my peace I give you in pieces and
pieces* but the gash turns everything ashen. I will not
recover, nothing, numb and dead. So—

when I kiss
your lips and break
the skin remember:

Not a single survivor to recount
our longing—it's hard to sleep in the Bermuda Triangle
(on the opposite
side, reports reversed)

in my letter
[

                                      ] lost
in the mails.

AT ITS CORE OPPOSITE LIES ANOTHER MORE
MYSTERIOUS—
                  *

The Bermuda Triangle is very likely a black
hole, we've gone missing—
transferred/transcribed/translated
straight through a worm hole—

                        spit out
                             Dragon side.
                 *

I still can't feel my pinky finger.
The dust in the field numbed
when fingertips brushed
even snow would not fall there, let alone
melt.

UPON THE FALL OF DIGITAL CABLE AND AFTER A WEEK
OF CLASSIC RERUNS, THE BROADCAST WILL RETURN
TO STANDBY—

*

My mouth a black whole also
Each word you send
reconstructed,
I emit these parcels:
inexplicable matter parsed,
something like gold dust—
rots faster.

*

I've just swallowed a bit of misinformation.
Plane food and pamphlets with escape diagrams
leave me a little _____   .

What resonates: flickers, end credits, voice-overs—
memories of you between
them all—

I am constructing my own survival guide.

FIND ANSWERS IN ELECTRIC SNOW—

*

I really did write but you know how things go
missing. Responses fall flat

escape
unnoticed.
(Something to do with reverse

magnetism and shipwrecks.)
We just can't get our bearings, I can't just—
and so grind my foot
into moondust.

We're all awash in the wreckage.

YET THE INTERIOR HAS BEEN EXPLORED IN OTHER
WAYS—

*

No, I am not in
disguise. Amelia Earhart is waving,
wiping away questionable histories
of failure to return to a given location or time.
For once, forget. Ignore
conspiracy theory.

STATIC, VIEWERS WILL BECOME PROPHETS FOR
LIMITED TIME/ONLY REVELATION IS SINGULAR—

*

In 2012 there is so much spewing
Brush my hand
again but careful
of my palm
(wormhole).

We become lava,
adorn collar bones with porphyry
and pumice stones.

In the Acceleration to Cosmological Constant More is Unknown than Known

Nikkita Cohoon

> He keeps swifts
> to feel the breath
> of flight, to bird love
> his transgressions.
>
> He tends them, keeps one eye
> on the sky that expands
> further than the breadth
> of a wing. Will keep expanding.
>
> He finds
> the truth in the rustle
> of the swifts, in wing's speculum,
> in trailing edge.
>
> When he fixes
> his telescope on an empty
> spot of sky, he shivers
> at the dark energy.
>
> He will still absorb the chill.

He keeps expanding
knows there is
not a point at which the universe falls
back in. Someday the swifts
and their long pointed wings will spread
and he won't be able
to plot them on a map.

He will be there when time is no longer marked by a clear
trajectory, when his own thoughts are cast so far out there won't
be a call to bring them back in again. He will witness the start
of the world's end. Nothing in the opening but black silence,
he will hinge his mouth wide enough for his jaw to crack: Note
migration patterns to measure time.

Live Stream: Apocalypse

Nikkita Cohoon

Predicted down to the minute by geologists or televangelists:

SEVEN MINUTES REMAINING

One live feed interrupted by a Skype call announcing the break of the 7th Seal.

On another website, the anchor person scoffs at a woman seen combing Hof Zikim, despite warnings that the white horse will first strike the seashore.

She'll be sorry.

THREE MINUTES REMAINING

Countless watch via broadband; the faithful promise to pray for the afflicted and eagerly await the countdown to see if faith will deliver.

TWO MINUTES REMAINING

Cut to a reporter live from 700 Club Headquarters. Pat Robertson promises to announce just as soon as God tells him anything conclusive. In the meantime, women with split ends should assume they are doomed.

FIVE MINUTES AFTER THE PREDICTED END

*Meredith Vieira is antsy. Pronouncements of relief are followed
by admonishments that the post-apocalypse may be worse than
the apocalypse itself.*

And the antichrist might be as attractive as Matt Lauer.

THIS STREAM WILL FADE—THE MEDIA WILL TRY
To wipe it.
    *Cut: the disappointment so evident on the faces of media
moguls when the apocalypse didn't*

    *Cut: the condescension for the unfaithful, the apathetic,
the indifferent*

    *Cut: the interview with the famous jockey (the only one
left with a website that could support enough bandwidth to
stream the video of the last thirty seconds)*

    Cut: the quote when one newscaster said,
                I can see the red horse just off to the left.

Spring

Kevin Duffy

Cold rain slaps at the windows.
Brubeck is down to a murmur.
She breaks the long silence:

"Daffodil Skilled Care. It sure didn't live up to the website."
"Yeah, like that place at Myrtle Beach."
"It's not funny."
"I know. I'm sorry."

The wipers
sweep away red and white moon craters,
to reveal sooted bungalows,
and umber brick cadavers, spray-can scrawled.
Home, to those black and white ghosts mugging over
longnecks,
in musty albums.

We didn't stay long.
Does it matter?
Amid the demented hallway shrieks,
and the stench of antiseptic and urine,
a woman, once beautiful and strong,
molder of generations,
sits oblivious in a stained flannel gown.

In the Middle

Sandra Feen

In the middle of seventh period teens
teacher centers herself on top
of student desk, tries to bridge
Shakespeare's blank verse
to words that float through
urban sensibilities.

Student raises her hand,
begins before teacher
acknowledges gesture, proper:
>*Why you sayin' shit*
>*that got nothin' to do*
>*with what's on this page?*
>*You be confusin' us and*
>*besides, you always talk*
>*about a bottom line, well*
>*here's mine: I don't care*
>*about no ideas of March—*
>*why should I?*

The bell rings.

It Is All

Sandra Feen

It is all she can do
to make bearable, first floor
for her eyes, others',
to vacuum soiled carpet
spot pale tile,
light bathroom, Yankee Harvest,
salvage purple
dried in corner ruby bud vase.
It is all she can
to erase shapes beneath
each ink bottle, dip
glass under water faucet
banish stacks, defer
beneath narrow dining
room cabinet.
It is all she
to prop estate doll
on rim of mahogany settle
felt arms casual,
cloth eyes steady
to revisit framed crocuses
to align rockers: polish moon.
It is all
to round the quiet house at night,
smell its dimly lit singular satisfaction.
It is
green's healing attempt:
color clarifies March coffee table
while upstairs chaos quakes.

"Beware the Ides of March," Says the Squirrel Swept up in the Talons of a Hawk

Charlene Fix

His tail is waving farewell like the tail of a kite
settling into a current when there's no holding it back—

he's on his way, his little camera eyes recording
a sweeping aerial shot, an establishing shot of spring—

forsythia fattening dooryards with butter flames,
ash whitening like bleached paper.

And inside the terror of the squirrel's happenstance proximity
to the hawk's predatory and awakened appetite,

is silence, like that between breaths at oval tables
where peace blooms after the hammering out.

For the hawk's feathered talons are gripping the squirrel's furred belly
so securely he knows he cannot fall,

and both accepted this moment back when their first cells
were reduplicating, the squirrel agreeing

to be a squirrel in the little-pear-womb of his chattering mother,
and the hawk agreeing to be a hawk inside the precarious egg.

But I: kingdomed, phylumed, haired, and wingless burning,
cannot assent, but watch their flight with bitter awe.

Fiasco Under an Impeccable March Sky

Charlene Fix

Today I'm trying to pick up my ninety-three-year-old mother
who is leaning on a cane waiting for me near the back door

of her eye doctor's office. But the city keeps rearranging its roads
until I end up in Gahanna, Hebrew, almost, for Hell.

There are many ways to reach the people we love,
but getting lost isn't one of them.

This fiasco unfolds like one of those dreams wherein whoops,
no clothes, and streets and buildings pull a semblance bait-and-switch

until you can't reach where you're trying to go. In waking life, a small
distilled self stands to the side, watching and lifting a brow,

confident of resolution though curious about how, before the Big
Kahuna of tomorrow washes the crisis away. Meanwhile,

it helps to have a cell phone and someone to call, in this case
a patient husband who has learned to filter hysteria and glean facts,

like the eye doctor's name. He looks up the number, but since
he isn't with me in the car, he doesn't hear hysteria's encore

when an office recording says they are closed for lunch.
My sister, however, later gets to pour a cup of tea and contemplate

my Hindenburgian bulletins on her answering machine from I-670 East
and I-270 South, from Sunbury and Mock Road, and sundry ravines

in between, describing how all of my efforts to reach our mother
are taking me further away from her: how roads, malls, suburbs, ramps,

and intersections are flinging themselves around until I suspect
it's the revenge of the itching oats buried in this former farmland.

The Fingers of Persephone

Charlene Fix

It is the same old wound that opens every spring,
last year's leaves on gustatory ground,
sudden robins tripping into view, their breasts
not blood red but the red of dialectic, rust.

The wound, uncauterized, stays fresh and doesn't ache
beneath the snow. And it is soothed by barren
trees with leafless arms, its own correlative:
the architecture of a comatose estate.

But now the fingers of Persephone crack earth,
and now the nearly almost lost return
in concert with a grand conspiracy of seeds
and spores and bulbs. Shoots sashay naked in the sun.

Making Love During a Terrorist Attack

Kate Fox

For RF

Auden was only half right; the truth is we must love
one another and die, which could explain why the move
to disrobe and lie, belly to belly—even while the world
collapses around us and the bodies of so many, like pearls,

are instantly crushed to dust—suddenly becomes imperative.
After all, we have never been ones to assume grief
can be so easily disentangled from love, that the ragged cry
of desire couldn't just as well be mistaken for the high

keen at the graveside. Still, better to believe our bodies can't
be broken by the weight of certain loss, that the slant
of light we catch so casually from the corner of our eye
can't possibly carry the method of our death. Which is why

on this exquisite September afternoon, as the sky erases
the mark of every contrail, and dust settles on the faces
of those sent to recover what we fear is lost forever,
we hold on to what we can, a worthy, if vain, endeavor.

"What Are You Prepared to Do?"

Kate Fox

> *"God help us if we all get what we deserve."*
> *-James Wright defending "At the Executed Murderer's Grave"*

It's already 80 degrees in southeastern Ohio on the first
                                        Monday of May,
and you are wondering if that scene in *The Untouchables* could
                                        ever really play out—
the one where Elliot Ness bluffs the judge, who orders the
                                        bailiff to switch juries

so that the other twelve, bribed by Al Capone, won't find him
                                        innocent. This,
because you are on the Grand Jury, and the lawyers who could
                                        answer your question
keep prompting the foreman to repeat "Do you swear?" and
                                        "So help you God?"

so many times the words lose their meaning. Bound by oath,
                                        you feel the weight
of Jim Malone's question gathering speed on the rails of blood
                                        left along the floor
as he drags himself from the back door to the parlor to retrieve
                                        the train schedule.

You find yourself mired in what you might do, if called upon
                                        right now, right
here, where it is against the law to jerk the dead to their feet
                                and kill them again,
where the baby in the pram will not be saved by the perfect aim
                                of the Italian cop,

where the reptilian killer will never be pushed from the
                                courthouse roof
for the sake of an audience that applauds as the street rushes up
                                to meet him,
the laws of gravity taking precedence over the court's best efforts.

Carciofi alla Romana

Jennifer Hambrick

The scent of her own perfume
mixes sweet with pino grigio,
in candle glow she looks
across the table, falling
into the furrow that cuts
between his eyebrows
as he speaks of nights
with someone else.
Her eyes drop to her plate
as his words flow into the stream
of music, hushed chatter
at other tables –
how mercifully sharp
the chef's knife must have been
to strip away calloused leaves
quick and clean,
to slice out those inner bristles
that, left in, only stir up heartache,
and leave the tender heart
unscathed, anointed with oil
and seasoned
as a fragrant offering.

Conspiracy

Jennifer Hambrick

Julia's ten-year-old antennae twitched when one day Cassie's
clique started including her in everything they did at school.
For three days the posse complimented the same clothes that,
Julia vividly remembered, two weeks earlier they had ridiculed.
They vied each other for the seat next to Julia at lunch. In gym
class Cassie even picked Julie first for her dodgeball team.
On day four one of Cassie's henchmen passed Julia a note in
social studies class. Letters gouged into the pulp of wide-ruled
paper slithered across the page: "It's a joke," they said, "We're
dumping you. Hahaha." Julia crumpled the note as the teacher
droned on about Congress. She tried to swallow the lump tight-
ening her throat. She looked down at her hands and noticed
the red spots on the note that the paper's edge, sharp as a blade,
had drawn.

Age Warps

Terry Hermsen

Age warps like a kind lover, her head
in the hollow of your shoulder. She feels
so good there after her long journey
across the globe. You're here, caving in
along a line of demarcation you immediately
ceded to her touch. She has the eyes of a child.
In them you watch the ship of your face
sail off and skirt the shoals. Foghorns
repeat the same chords as yesterday,
their johnny-one-note melody you begin to hum.

**

Age warps the walls. The dozen steps
up to the porch you deconstruct in segmented
breaths. Who were you at the base, or gazing
out the windows? Daily you lay out the charts
of your confessions, compose your absolutions
in the absence of the judge, the failed
architect. The tape measure? It's spun
back on its loop of darkening numbers, loose measurements
for a cheek bone, an aural canal growing hollow.
Add the separations, concave losses whose arc
of sums forms a clasp, a kiss, another face.

**

Age warps. Refusing descent. Blood in the cup,
tiny scales for the jeweler's eye. We disappear
down lenses, parading pronouns, grasp mostly
the knobs to the same old rooms. But here the blind
are scraping back their sight, the sentences hovering
in corners with their ticker-tape machines. Nots unknot
and wrap your shoulders with all you never learned.
And it is she again. Here beside you.

Fractal Walk

Terry Hermsen

For Alice Fulton

On the stage, half-constructed for the last production
blue lines shoot out to help the actors imagine

the universe. Why am I, before the carpenters arrive,
the hunter of wisdoms, counter-sinking into my mind the bolts

of this man-made cliff? (I'd always rather've been on the stage crew.)
Plumb lines arrange the stars to seek a way out of silence.

So much room when looking out from the stage.
So narrowed the eyes of the audience.

———

Before the staggered stairs of the apartment house on Plum
I sit among seeds of a myriadic maple.

White stucco. Lurid irises with their folded-over tongues.
You fix your screen door, #10, with sheets of plastic

and strips of white tape. And these must be
your bedroom curtains with floating smiling skulls.

———

Clock shop – weights and faceless hammers –
pendulums at different earthly paces

inside of glassed half-opened hearts.
When I could barely see, I thought I could make out

the seconds moving on the red quivering
measuring hand that was school.

Surely the hereditary clock repairman
waits inside his grandfather's beard.

He does not   worry too much
  about his reflection   in the darkening sundial.

———————

  Abandoned Shinto shrine –   is it empty now
or full of us?   And are there voices

that are required   for silence
or must we   become blossoms?

No matter how many times   I shake the branch,
there's always one   that falls too late.

———————

  Museum   of the Underground
    tucked into the neck   of the library.

  Traced in blue-print: Africa Road
down the center   of Ohio.

 Three velvet roses   at the carriage house window
tell how many   for dinner tonight

Twenty years later, a village   of the freed
 given the name   of a continent.

  In a hundred,   the bulldozers
    choose this swarm of houses   to drown for a dam.

  No photos in these drawers   of you, viney graves.
When you were buried   under a hundred feet of concrete

 no one could look   down into your walls.
There were too many   surging voices

to hear them all   inside the singing water –
 and the names   that keep on walking.

Mark Rothko, "Red Maroons" (1962)

Terry Hermsen

```
                    ashen core
        body down              wide coffin
        lay this               door - how
  bored of boundaries          can I shape
        how can I              my falling
     grate of sound            division whole
        slumber               narrow verge
        rainborn              verse lip tongue
wordscar storm                 swallow
    umber valence             flight mortem
        throne                slipped column
        coupled               vicious nitches
      open favor              eastern pallor
     jostled stone            loose house
          leaden quarry    fade and turn
                 tomb or chapel
```

Mondays, Wednesdays, Fridays

Krista Hilton

the Denver homeless wait behind St. Paul's
for eleven o'clock and free sandwiches.
I take this shortcut, measuring my steps,
not too fast, not too slow, not
wanting to draw attention to
the briefcase banging my thigh.
More men than women stand in line,
more blacks than Hispanics, more
Hispanics than whites.

As the months pass, not knowing why,
I walk closer, near enough to hear
their voices, what the sandwich is,
which shelter has open beds, which take kids,
the last place Joe was seen this week.
They pay no attention to me, just another
somebody who's got somewhere to go, who's got
a schedule to keep that's got nothing
to do with standing in their line.

One day, hurrying toward food,
a man runs into me; we both stop.
I wonder if he thinks I'm one of them;
blowing snow makes it difficult to see.
We stand close. Whiskey breath, damp wool coat,
briefcase between our knees,
leather shoes next to Michael Jordans.
I turn to go, but he grabs my arm,

looks me full in the face, his eyes clear.
You come by here all the time, he says. I nod.
Where you going? I tell him; he nods,
except now he's a bobble head doll,
clarity gone, eyes unable to focus,
mouth opening, shutting, speaking air.
I hurry away knowing he's unlikely to recall
our exchange. But I will, so much so
I never walk down that street again.

In the Middle of That Night

Chad Jones

For Tank

Hours after witnessing a man
with scarred hands drain life
from the family dog,
I swept dead leaves out
from the garage, convinced
his suffering was traded for ours.
Too late for whiskey,
too early for coffee,
sleep played hide and seek
as I paced the kitchen, bothered by
a brown-speckled banana, begging
to be removed from its miserable skin.

Careful not to disturb
the quiet of an empty house,
I inched towards the window
to pacify the silence
of the wind's pursed lips,
digging in my pocket to offer
the gesture of smoke
and a flick of light,
only to find a silver chain
and a crumpled note,
unsigned, and thankful
that the fear didn't get in the way.

Shaking hands with this
news, I found myself
tired, but waited up
for an old friend,
one who knows even more
about death, who dies every night,
only to rise, daily, always
shedding light, over the cancerous
darkness of those nights.

Rubicon

Mark Sebastian Jordan

I wish I could file you away.

But it's like listening to
a favorite piece of music:
Even after a hundred spins,
my ears overturn new things,
and I wonder how I missed
those strands, those relationships.

Time doesn't lessen pain,
it just puts it further down the road.
But if all roads lead to Rome,
then you were its empire,
and some nights Tchaikovsky
drives me over the Rubicon of time
and I gather my legions, prepared to march
and seize what should rightly be mine.

Somewhere around dawn,
I remember your husband,
sweet and sane and good for you,
not to mention your baby boy,
and I dismiss my gall.

Yet I shall always believe you spend
some portion of every day
eyeing the Appian Way
in case your heart should flutter
like a distant regimental flag
snapping in the noonday sun.

Crop-Dusting in a Rickety Plane in Shaky Weather & as Enhanced by the Unbearable Nature of Your Daze & the Miles-of-Nothingness Feast of Late

Ariana-Sophia Kartsonis

Oh Precious, kerosene early spring,

torch the month of March, immolate the deep

cicada sleep unravelling below us

even as we don't speak. My sing-along

song goes I want you buried in the yard

& don't think it means nothing, the double

negative weather, the double bed fiasco,

the ding-a-ling of old alarm clocks

& your heart thumping up from the garden

where someone has planted mango

portalaca & bell peppers, Queen

Sophia marigolds to keep vigil

over the plain tomato which no one dare

call a love apple this week. Oh Peach-pit

who will pinch the flea beetles nibbling

on your good sense. If you hear in me

now someone you don't want to know, blame

the unsound map you packed in the red

jalopy, the German bitch you call your ride.

The world war too we keep inside, the soldiers

beating down our doors. There's nothing more
to do but wait for harvest-time. Until
then, be sure you're sure of what
you're pulling up from the roots before
it's in your grip, before it's tossed aside.
& if I were you I'd wear
a carnation in the buttonhole
of the left breast pocket of the bluebird
shirt where you used to keep our hearts, so that
laying down on any plot of ground you'll
still seem like the one from whom flowers
grow right through.

Frank O'Hara I Love You!

Ariana-Sophia Kartsonis

Let's walk from here to that taxi-stand
reading the city like a sonnet.
You're the man, after all, to bring on
poems playing down my xylophonic spine
You make me want to drop handkerchiefs,
drop hints, check into a hotel with someone
I'm wearing my heart like a ski mask
and I want to take this whole city
in and pawn it for Manhattan in a soap dish
and you—the cakiest boy-loving form
of complimentary bliss
in justrighttight jeans—have me in a lather. This soapdish
city, this poem ain't big enough for the both of us,
March in, lionesque, March out, Lamb.
You are the tears in my teacup
and Frank, I drink you up.

Pettifog: The Scientist and the Troubadour Collide

Ariana-Sophia Kartsonis

"Why do you insist on presenting a deliberately inaccurate
depiction of the events?"
Because the moon just now is a porthole into a beyond world,
a hole punched by drunk angel into a heaven as a Walmart
fluorescent light pooling up from the other side.
It isn't that I don't know better, don't understand the hard science
negates the possibility of the moon as a meringue pie
meant to be lemon but filled instead with fireflies,
it's that the what-ifs mean more to me than the "where
were yous on the night in question?" Not because I would lie
but because I would rather lie down with you and look
at such a sky because for-the-best though it may be,
there are no good reasons for not letting me lie.

Apology to the Oracle

Matt Kilbane

> *The greatest blessings come from madness,*
> *indeed of madness heaven-sent*
> *—Plato*

Late summer at Delphi, the sky
a storm drumming the west horizon.

Clocking-out, she pitches off
her stool of three ivory legs. Gold fumes—

petrochemical, we know now,
an ethylene—rise still

from the child-size rift
in the marble floor. Hers has been

a 16 hour shift. She can feel the god
inside her, warming with a god's hands

each sore bone. He'll stay
as long as waking does, waiting

for sleep, should it ever come,
to shoulder him out. In the day's

last prophecy, a prospective matricide
broke a young man so, he tore

his own ear off, tossed the red coin
into her lap of beads. It's a business

best left to women worn
by a forgivable desire for history, history

in its sheep clothes; forgivable,
perhaps, because you too have broken

midnights with your waking, have poured
milk in the dark of your dark kitchen,

and with wet lips asked
for something like assurance she tried

her best to see that invisible body
held always out of reach before you,

for something like her
drugged eyes closed.

Il Risorgimento

Matt Kilbane

In its first line the poem said
heart cry, cry
of the lonely heart. We read it
breathless beside the stone Garibaldi
in Washington Square.
At the free clinic where
you work, a patient, a man
you'd never seen before
borrowed from you a looseleaf
piece of paper. For a poem,
he said, for you.
The shuddering you felt, that odd
and fierce blessing, when he,
laughing, tucked
the folded, finished poem
into your white coat's pocket—
my own heart vicariously
skips a beat. Garibaldi,
retreating after
much brave resistance
into the Italian countryside, said
to his weary men:
wherever we may be, there

is Rome. It is easy—as easy as
imagining his billowing
red shirt in the dry
wind, his flashing saber—easy
to believe that no one
believed him, that most scoffed
or snickered as they watched
their city sieged, then
sacked. That his silly metaphor
fell completely flat. It is easy,
and love is not.

In Which I Find Myself in the Middle

Matt Kilbane

The wonky, braying *walk* sign's buzzer
as red hand convalesces to green
striding man on the corner of Pierce and O'Connell—

corner of your chapped lip's superb traction
in the shade of a blue beech, Raquel,

and at dawn the mulish return
of a half-burnt votive ship. You drawling
in delivery of the *Vita Nuova*, before vomiting

seven salsa jars of Popov and Pepsi. I said sin tax,
not syntax. "No More Parents,

No More Gods," versus the finer teeth
of Duns Scotus. The historical personage
Kenny Chesney, as opposed to his amaranthine song,

and the subtle ravishment stuttering
across your wind-raw (top's down) face, en route

to my brother's BBQ, Memorial Day, '08.
I'm at the corner of who

you still are, probably, and how I'm probably

wrong. Of a flushed, daybroken bedroom
window, and that votive ship again,

me climbing in—it sounds like a crack
shot in the laser tag we often played,
those nights you let me win,

this wonky, braying *walk* sign's buzzer.

Hip Bone Connection

Gail Martineau

Pop.
First thing in the morning and
First thing before I give in to sleep.
Sometimes, they wake me in the night—wake my partner—
To remind me of my day
Sitting on my sit bones.

The hurt wasn't there once.

Before driving, before my real job, before being a grown-up.
Somersaults, crawling, sitting on my knees.
Easy as pie.

Expansion.
Fifty pounds lighter and I still wouldn't be able to fit in those
jeans again.
That's what they do as a woman ages. Turns into a real woman.
They're meant for babies, for slamming car doors shut, for
flirting, for showing some attitude.

Those sit bones sure do hurt.

Brotherhood

Alexis Misko

The older man's
whiskey eyes squint scan
over my body
and out peeking comes
his sweat tongue:

"Hey gal,"
fumbles mid-air but
his hands on the small
of my back squirming say,
"Let me suck your tits
'cause that's all you are
on top them black boots
is a pair of tits."

I move instead
toward the younger man
room's opposite side
but his palm chooses reckless
abandon grazing over
the back pocket
of my jeans.

No solace found
in the bartender's complacent smile
when I order
a rum and diet with lime
and on his shirt he blots
the dripping juice
from his fingers.

Lines Written at a Red Roof Inn While Watching a Movie About John Dillinger

Nathan Moore

To avoid grief cultivate
debt. To be in debt is to drag
a cursor over celebrities
who wear inappropriate
swim trunks.

Multiple media feature
faces made of angles. Keep ganglia
clean, cursors cleaner.
To avoid suspicion wear
men's clothes.

To avoid the law be racked by a crucial
cry. The law is email.
When the law bends down, ear-to-mouth,
listening for some last words, shake
all strength out and bite.

Navigational Metrics

Nathan Moore

I lose faith in the printed word
until I read my obituary

quietly to myself in a room
organized around a chair's

personality in an atmosphere
nourished by shock that refuses

to thread snow's painful blur

with the challenge of anesthetized
flight over aestheticized landscapes.

My neighbor's silver maple breaks over his ice-bearing Accord.
Tracks on dusted asphalt are printed branches.

For now, measure touch. Later, prancing retinas.

When Senators Attack

Nathan Moore

All my Facebook friends hate me.
A vivid sense of historical greed, combined with an enthusiasm
for marble, signals
the approach of some bearded human
who mouths "I'm acquainted with vibrations."
Some lip-cleaned mug brim lifted over a desktop
of unshuffled paperwork: someone at the Statehouse
hunts a dirty interpretation. Someone on The Force
chalks the sharp outline of a monstrosity.
"You too, bro? Don't tase me!"
The enemy of absence is whatever.
I am one of thousands to hail a judgment.
The pill swamp lulls my stab wound. The mother
of all newspapers issues my permission slip.
Entering as a lie, I leave a lamb chop.

Meteoric

Brad Pauquette

The Senator hoofs towards me, heavy on his heels.
The September sun assaults us, I in the huddled, beseeching masses,
he an evolving rill carving its way through the heaving crowd.
Photons of light embed in the dense fiber of his wool suit coat,
like parasites,
leeches gnawing at his pores, sucking out the cold—
gnawing, preying, feigning symbiosis.

He reaches for my hand, holding it firmly between both of his.
His hands are greased, like vaseline, a snail melting under a salt shower,
slimy, iridescent streaks staining the brick.
The sweat from his palms congeals into orbs amidst the grease,
like ball bearings between the surfaces of our skins,
microscopic gel capsules of likeability.

"Thank you for your support," he says, quietly as if the
message is just for me.
I heard him mutter the same thing to the woman three rows
down and two columns over
and to the man two rows down and one column over.
But now I'm certain, it's just for me.
I mumble something between "Thank you" and "You're
welcome" through frozen lips, sawdust tongue
But he has already glided onward towards a woman six
outstretched hands down.

I watch him as he moves, his eyes focus, shift, focus, shift—
a thousand personal contacts an hour, ten thousand swoons a day.
Packed on grease and dry heated, like beef jerky,
the Senator a fatty, bloated treat for the masses, sweet and salty.
The label swears he'll taste so good, promises smooth digestion,
two hundred artificial ingredients listed on the bottom of his shoe.

The photons steal his energy, leeching it by miniscule attrition.
But with every piercing stare, every nod, every boyish grin,
his palms absorb more than he loses.

I came to take, but I only give.

Decision Maker

Cynthia Rosi

We are arrows shot
black against turquoise sky
a silver-tipped swish.

We, the bow,
the burning bicep
white-tipped fingers, blood starved,
hot scrape of string to arm
and the vibrating core
of the bow-master.

In my quiver, a thousand decisions;
aim of my eye,
each shot, destiny wrought.

The arc interrupted by an act of will, or not
interrupted at all.

Judas and Brutus on Time in the Ninth Circle

Alexis-Rueal

It isn't the fire—
you get used to the fire,
get used to it eating away the flesh,
only to see it grow back again.
Interesting process, really, except
that it takes such a long goddamn time.
The old man calls this "child's play."
Leave it to the murderers and thieves
to wail at fire's petty ways.
No, that wily bastard gave us something
special—each other.

An eternity of each other's company—
eyes prying away the sins fire refuses to burn off,
voices that speak in the language of the betrayed.
An eternity of "Et, tu?" licked deep into the ear,
of lips pressed to cheeks, of silver and knife
melded to hand palm.

No arguing why we did what we did—
trying to defend ourselves just leads to
tongues eaten out of heads by hounds.
Took a millennia for our tongues
to grow back obedient.
Speak when spoken to and say
only what he wants you to say.

We asked him what he wanted from us
that first day.
Old man didn't miss a beat,
"I want your denial burnt to ash.
I want you to be a walking accusation,
walking condemnation.
I want you to be nothing
but what you have done."
We didn't understand, were too
pissed off to see past our own self-pity.

It's been too long, though.
We wear our sins in place of skin.
It's natural to us, now.
We are nothing but our betrayals—
And that knowing hurts like hell.

Heart Attack Suite

Barbara Sabol

Small gnaw in the wall, amplified by the hollow cauldron
of 3 AM or by the mind at work on a line, a rhyme, and there it was
again: menace tap, a tick ticking—needles knitting from a skein
of web and wire in the intramural space between bedroom and den.

For years I lived with the quick, livid sound, the persistent click,
a feral tympani. It clotted the wall with an irregular cadence
of sharp body parts: nail, bone, teeth. Shirring of leather-
sheathed wings, furred belly chapping plaster.

I'd adjust the volume, pull the cover higher to shroud the sound.

I never pondered what loves the dark, what does its close,
wrought work in shadowed corridors; not until the winged flutter
beat like the devil, stunned, one bright-lit afternoon,

on a simple walk. Out of the blue, an animal knowledge
of what fills the space between wall and all else.

Nyx

Barbara Sabol

The drenched air suddenly wing-shuffled—
the Red Wing's abrupt tumbling call. You realize
you've been listening for the blackbird's hark,
its familiar trill. Voice of an intimate, come back.
Turn and turn, search the grey landscape—quicken
to Nyx who cracks the dark void, marrying sky to earth.

The Lakota hear the Red Wing's cry as *Oh! That I might die!*
To die while the memory of push and crown, root, stalk,
thrum of sap into the tub, clenches in the chest.
The great swirl circles counterclockwise—milkweed recast
as seed in the waiting pod, in the thrall of unbecoming.

On the brink of this obsolete lock, you watch the sluggish water
pulse with return: toad rouses from the mud bank, black snake
unribbons from her suspended life, warms her blood below
on the crumbling pudding stone wall.

To die in the middle of miracles when the rusted wheel
might turn again, sluice in the flow and sweep you
onto the thawing chest of water, into the creaturely colors
of the season. Oh to be lifted off this lock into the weightless
hands of March wind, while the earth drinks in the sky's blue
and heaven swims green with river, river.

Thirteen Ways of Looking at Yarrow

Barbara Sabol

After Wallace Stevens

I
Among three spring meadows
the only movement
was a shiver of yarrow.

II
I was of 100 minds
like a field
in which there are countless stalks of yarrow

III
The wave of yarrow in the autumn winds
was a pantomime of harp, of white caps

IV
A woman and her dog
are One.
A woman and her dog and a field of yarrow
are One.

V
Which is more wondrous—
the beauty of a woman's voice at dusk,
the open throat of hidden meanings,
yarrow rustling in a long breeze
or just after?

VI
The cold breath of winter
frosts the parlor windows.
The memory of hundred leaves grass
reflected on the glass;
or is it the lace collar
of an imagined woman?

VII
O pale men of Akron,
why do you imagine red hibiscus?
Can't you see how the yarrow
swirls around the ankles
of the women about you?

VIII
I know the hawk's call, wild
accents, and the river's hymn;
I know, too,
that a field gone to yarrow knows
more than all I know.

IX
The starling gathers yarrow
to line her nest; nearby,
a circle of white clusters bows.

X
When constellations of light
dart above the meadow, ghosting
the yarrow beneath
even the second tier of sky cries out!

XI
She rode across Ohio
on a glass bicycle
and when weariness overcame her
she mistook a field of yarrow
for a feather bed

XII
The yarrow is circling
the grave of Annie Oakley

XIII
Morning and night gather
together with the blackbird
on a white quilt of yarrow.

Good Friday: Ellicottsville, IN

Sherri B. Saines

Three church carillons
triangulate my backyard
with 19th century dirges.
The Catholics on the hill;
The Methodists on Main;
The Presbys on Front
take turns at 3:00.

I know all the words.

Beneath the cross of Jesus
Low in the grave He lay
Washed in the blood of the Lamb

I am collapsed here in the grass
to let the Spring sun dry
pneumonia from my lungs,
just warm enough in late day to rest
spread-eagle with the wounded.

I've been nowhere else in days.
I breathe though a brick
and cough through mud.
The drugs give me the runs.

Allergic apostate to the holiness of Spring
even the smell of pear blossom
breathes like cold gravy.

Were you there when they crucified my Lord
Hath not our Savior grief and tears

Were I well
I would charge up that catholic hill
and demand respite from their bells.
For God's sake
some of us know
all the words.

Handling Death

Jack Schwarz

I stoop to lift a freshly grounded starling,
And stroke this stricken bit of fallen sky,
Abruptly undone by marble wall and concrete walk.
Its still, still-warm, unflighted, songless body
Cannot be roused, or launched, revived, or healed.

Death can be handled, after all –
Not managed, or tamed, or sent packing,
Not coaxed into decorum,
But held –
Not held accountable, or in check;
Neither held back, nor corralled in the wings,
But clasped –
Cupped by grieving palms,
Gravely cradled.
Death can be handled, after all –
Not comprehended, but grasped.

I hold this downed life, this broken beauty,
Caress the iridescent feathers that now are
Death's own nest.
I place the bird, the never-again bird,
Inside an open garbage bin,
Atop a lidless, sauce-stained pizza box,
Beside a dented cola can,
Next to a coupon just expired.
And I pray that Death will be handled,
One last time:
Smothered by mounds of unfinished meals,
Broken bottles and soiled napkins;
Buried alive in an aerie of refuse,
Flightless forever.

Pleated Heart

Jack Schwarz

The purple iris I have not betrayed
If by the yellow, too, I'm captivated.
Affections to each other are related,
Just as sunlight is connected to the shade.

To primrose and to lily both I'm loyal;
The charms of neither do I take for granted.
In one glad heart their images are planted;
Both thrive in that invigorated soil.

Every passion's seeded by the past,
And blossoms from what hearts already hold.
Each fresh devotion fortifies the old,
And each new love's a tribute to the last.

Winter Offering: Turning Forty

Jack Schwarz

Birthday-wrapped in tangled folds of self,
Lost inside my own December cloth,
I felt a penetrating chill take hold.
Beyond me was the river, also seized by Winter's talons,
Beleaguered by its predatory claws.
And yet, although encased by frigid crust, a nascent shell,
The current flexed and struggled mightily to flow.
Abruptly, crystal skies released a gift:
The gulls emerged,
Wings gleaming whiter even than the dropping snow.
They wheeled, and dipped, and dove amid the flakes,
A sea-born benediction gliding in descent,
A sky-spawned act of grace on inland ice.
My birthday gulls alighted and assembled on the floe,
Rigid and attentive candles set ablaze by sun,
Poised in shining expectation of my wish.

Bad Key

Natalie Shapero

Copy of a copy, see the rut?

Nothing's born that way.
How do you think I got to be where I am today?

It shows on my face. I'm all turned down,
ill-suited to the lock of it,

the whole unluck of me.

With doors, if you can't see the hinges, it's a push.
Heavy ones you do

with both hands. Which is the way
God doesn't give.

Lean Time

Natalie Shapero

Without is how I go. The best defenses
fluctuate in scope and in supply.
The price of attack dogs now is very high.
I've hidden my old love's letters in a bag.
Reading one is eating from the trash.
In the dream I heard his actual laugh.

Outcasts only care what outcasts think.
I gather together the people I have hurt
and rate them. Lover's hair, like a red shirt
washed with a white shirt. Nobody can
forgive. I hate them, and they hate me back.
In the dream I heard his actual laugh.

It's often said, of eating from the trash,
that many women do it. You have slammed
the lid, but then again, it's diet be damned
and what a waste. Fries in a paper sack,
dirty from coffee grounds. I almost gagged.
In the dream I heard his actual laugh.

Spare Me

Natalie Shapero

thin displays of self-rely, cake
you've learned to make over

an open fire, lock

you're picking over an open
fire, fire you're starting

over an open fire.

The sheep ate everything
off the drying line. I had to lie

about the sweaters

so as not to call a creature
a cannibal, acrylic all,

I swear it. Why

do farm boys bring their sheep
to the edges of cliffs?

It's the only way

to make the sheep
push back. I took a while

to get that one.

I took a while to send myself
so far there were no phones

to wait by. I fell silent.
Sheep are easiest to clone

because they are natural

followers. In wartime,
so the gardeners could enlist,

Woodrow Wilson grazed

a dozen sheep on the White
House lawn. It worked out fine.

The meek, the Earth,

assess the signs. I'm living
off crab apple scraps. They said

I was too quickly

hurt. Believe me, I have
been called worse.

All three of Natalie Shapero's poems were first printed in No Object,
and are reprinted with permission.

Botany in the Underworld

Hannah Stephenson

Imagine that the woods will end here
and then they do, dropping off along
a cliff. You put it there, the cliff, the woods,
every moth sailing down like debris
from an explosion overhead. You can
fill an entire field with forget-me-nots,
with the same forget-me-not over and over,
blue with a purple stain on one petal.
The trees are all familiar because you chose
them, pear blossoms like fog spooled
in the branches. When you encounter a plant
you do not know, you are settling in here.
The framework of the Underworld is communal,
we all contribute to its structure, farmers.
If you miss a season, for instance, autumn,
put it out into the world. I guarantee
that someone else is missing autumn, too.

It Is in the Knife

Hannah Stephenson

It is in the knife to split substance.
It is in the knife to seize the magnet.

The paradox: saw the bread in half,
now there are two pieces. Division

and multiplication make similar
products: more stuff. Look at your

impulse to cut, look out for it.
Hack at the thing and you have

copied it. Recall your last haircut,
how as you left you stepped over

piles of strands, strewn thick as hay.
All that hair was reaped from your head,

from what still hangs thick from
your scalp. As disintegrating of a force

as it may be, the blade replicates.
The knife was born to cleave

and cling. From its teeth, edges
emerge, freshly-forged perimeters.

You Knew What I Was When You Picked Me Up

Hannah Stephenson

Don't carry the snake up the freakin'
mountain, kids. Even if he asks nice.
Even if he is old, if he squints at you
like your cat does. Don't tell him
your name. If he says your mom sent
him, ask him for the password. If he
doesn't say hamburger hamburger,
get out of Dodge. Don't look like you
are alone. Hint that your parents are
near, just not available. He doesn't need
your help. He can cross the river fine.
He can rock climb fine. Your backpack
is not a snake carrying case. His fangs
can get at your skin through canvas,
through leather, through denim. If he
says his fangs are dentures, he's lying.
If he says his venom's all dried up,
he's lying. He might tell you that
humans are his favorite. That he
once had a little boy who was his
friend. They would hike up hills
and go swimming together, snake
riding zipped up in the chest of

the boy's hooded sweatshirt, snake
resting little snake chin on the zipper.
Even if he says he's not a rattlesnake,
he could be. Even if you shake him
hard and don't hear a thing. Trust
your fear, kids. It's not enough to
leave him once you've found him.
He's gonna keep talking to you in
that smooth, scaly voice, telling you
it's ok, he doesn't want to hurt you,
he just wants to sunbathe. Even as a
snakelet, he is dangerous. We are
not trying to scare you. You need to
hear this. There are snakes everywhere.
Even a baby snake is a snake. Don't
let him talk. You don't want to get bit.

Another Storm Poem

Jordy Lawrence Stewart

we gargled over the hump in the
crossing that slid us into federal road.
the old car kicked down a gear as
i was offered one more cigarette.
every time i light one up i think of
every time i've heard *I don't know*
why I smoke these things, they're nasty.
they were nasty and i didn't know
why i smoked them. rolling cigarettes
was the busiest activity in riverside.

the snow couldn't wait for november.
it fell in a gracious flurry in front of
the headlights—snow—snow is attached
to many things, but it didn't stick to
the road that night. it stuck in my mind
and i felt winter's venom leaking into
my bones, into my blood, filling my mind.
love and resentment are a different flip
of the same coin. the air blew into the
window pushing back the ashes glowing
in contrast of the fruitless fields full of
hard dirt and the long gone harvest vibration.

some stalks danced across the old country
road and looked like ghosts and loneliness.
i watched them rolling in between reflectors.
punk rocked blared all the way back to town.
i didn't listen to it. i heard it like another
riff in the howling wind that swayed the car.
the hurricane to the east had made its way,
and in its exhaust, i was in a car in the dark,
leaving company, the smoke, the drink, the
silly laughter of light headed jabbering-ons.

i carefully let my cigarette out the window,
watched it take flight to disappear into the cold.
i didn't know what i'd do tomorrow or the day after,
probably think about the storm, think about tonight
and hopefully then, think about nothing.

waiting in bed for another hurricane.

A Hallway Poem

Joy Sullivan

Serious questions, all concave mewing.
What kind of dewiness winks out of the frame?
Portrait and Glitz.

I look. I open my skin.
Wet, we glow darkly.
Pressure and discarded mirth.

Earnest origins,
as if you only wanted to know only
one small truth well

but felt the books were lying—
they stacked into each
other with such cozy misery. It ate up

the peach pit of your heart.
The lights switched on,
you burned like a village.

My Hips Quaked & You

Joy Sullivan

blossomed out,
child spangled with blood,
corkscrew for a heart.
Women will invent stories
to keep you in at night.

A flower evolved to smell like rotting meat.

Hordes of fresh flies madden at its fragrance. Wrapped by a
spathe, the lucid genealogy of plants

a single carpel, holy communion
quiet bread, savage flesh.

Percussion (re)

Joy Sullivan

There are two dogs in the yard. One is howling the other silent.

Why does silence exist?

Because you are full
of non-words.

What is a non-word?
It is word eaten by the listener.

As if we were children. Seen and not heard.

Let me grow older with you.
We pass through anything we do not anticipate.

A dog in the yard sees a shadow
begins to growl.

We muzzle it.

Tender

Dameion Wagner

When I feel like a dried chicken bone
ready to crack and splinter, or
brittle sandpaper that's been wetted
and dried, wetted and dried, or
a throat that's parched and gagging,

I imagine it all like baking topsoil.

I want to get into my car and
drive, drive, drive:

There's something to be said for being honest
with someone else. But doesn't it say more
when I'm honest with me?

If my car bent itself into or around or
through or behind, into shards of
cartilage and marrow, burgundy and
full of rot,

it would not be so bad, I suppose.

Tornado Sirens

Dameion Wagner

My mom was late that
night. Ham, corn,
potatoes au gratin; milk,
bread, applesauce; good
china, stainless flatware.
(An empty place setting.)

Even at twelve I had
an awful sense that
something bad was
happening; I didn't have
the language for it. I
heard my dad through
his lips, pulled

straight: "Who were you
with?" That heavy question.
Like the green, still sky
before a tornado. I didn't
know where to take shelter.

If You Think There Is Nothing for You Here

Scott Woods

There is a woman -
I do not know what she is saying -
who hangs a picture of her lover
at the edge of a coal mine where he is trapped.
Weeks. Darkness. Juggling.
I do not understand her prayers.
I do recognize the universal symbol for "come to me."
She cries every day in the same spot.
His wife has torn down her pictures and slapped her
once for each time Jesus' name spilled from her lips.
Her face is swollen and plum from this.
This is the only story I want to know about.
I have made coffee to this story,
dipped a heart, rich, into the hills,
a bleeding croissant.
They do not show her picture.
They show his. I do not know if it is hers.
When I think it is his wife's I add sugar.
When I think it is his lover's I add nothing.

If you think there is nothing left for you here,
kiss me for the first time again.
Who will you hug when you come out of that coal mine?
The you that is
has torn down my recollections
of the you that used to be
three times since it became clear
who my tears were for.
And I would kiss you still,
even with the lick of coal on your lips,
the ash of an impossible decision,
the breath of another lover in your mouth.

Mistaken

Scott Woods

What I say about you
I say about myself, but don't believe.
I say you are morning.
Only night rests in my jowls.
I say you are where poetry needs to go,
even though I know it is already there.

I could taste the ruins in your mouth,
where the men who planted flags on your breasts
discovered the person already living there,
called her "found."
The brick clay mission they made you build
in your belly is patched and crumbling,
yet your eyes still worship there,
still break wafers over their plates,
staring back into the distant past.
Feed me the cracker of your body
and wonder why I still hunger.

This is why your kisses tasted like
the song I have remembered all wrong,
danced to all wrong, filled the bar we talked in
with too much smoke and light.

So I say you are a construct.
I say you are not the chicken wings and
sausage and peppers or the pillow of your hair.
You are not the knot in the kerchief of Baldwin's throat,
not your moans that were mine
or the gravel piling up in your scars.
I have written so many odes to your scars
you have been rubbed smooth with tongue.

These things look back in a mirror at me
every morning you are not here.
The morning you never stayed to savor,
the here that you were never in,
the you that you never were.

To the High School Thug Who Broke into His English Teacher's Car

Scott Woods

What you know about Nina Simone
could do laps on a pencil tip,
so I'm struggling to understand
why you would steal that CD.

That you skipped the vodka in the glove compartment
but took my reading glasses is equally perplexing.

It's not my fault you can't handle grammar,
but it may be my fault it never took.
Allow me the honor of tutelage now:
Name the verb in the following sentence:

Nina Simone sings.

Not knowing what kind of grades you get in math,
let me point out that you have a 50/50 shot here.

What will you make of the ugly woman
who sings so sweetly from the bottom of her stories
that she becomes—beautiful?
That you long for her entreating loneliness in the night
and wonder why girls today can't do it like that anymore?

How will you explain the mourning tripping out
of your poster-covered bedroom and into the hallway,
making your momma wonder who got into her momma's
records?

Nina Simone knows who you are and why you took that,
why the record called to you when fear struck your senses.

Nina Simone sings and I know you don't understand yet
the ramifications of what you've done,
how getting kicked out of your English class doesn't make it
okay,

I know you couldn't possibly have conceived
that there are people in this world
who can show you their love in three notes.

You had no idea that some people need songs like that,
songs that reach through time and pull your heart down like
fire alarms and run through the hallways of your soul,
banging on the doors,
trying to get the demons to walk out civilly,
in a straight line just outside your mouth,
falling into a vodka double-shot you can't lift on your own.

I want to imagine you just like that:
sitting in your bedroom,
staring out a window cracked from your previous shenanigans,
headphones to your skull,

scanning liner notes in my reading glasses,
Nina Simone singing long and hard into the night,
after a moment of trifling anger,
to see a beautiful thing and imagine it could save your life,
sometimes,
like it does mine,
every time the moon hangs there like it's harvest time,
pregnant with mankind's wishes,
heavy with the sorrow of thieves.

Acknowledgments

This anthology, like all of Columbus Creative Cooperative's books, was a product of many hands, and we couldn't possibly thank each and every person who contributed to this work.

Thank you to all of the poets who submitted work for consideration for this anthology.

Thank you to our editors, Hannah Stephenson, and to this book's designers, Yao Cheng and Brad Pauquette, as well as all of the fine folks who have worked to turn this project into a reality.

Thank you to Paging Columbus and The Ohio State University Urban Arts Space for supporting the poetry community in Columbus.

Thank you to all of the members of Columbus Creative Cooperative who attended workshops to improve each other's work, who share links and forward emails to your family and friends, and who go out of your way to support CCC through the year.

Finally, thank you, dear reader. You're the reason we produce books. Without your support of our mission, and your decision to purchase a CCC book, we wouldn't be able to produce the work of Central Ohio writers.

Poet Biographies

Steve Abbott is a founding member and co-host of The Poetry Forum. He has received an Ohio Arts Council grant for poetry and an OAC residency in Provincetown, MA. His work has appeared in a range of literary journals and anthologies. In 2008, he edited *Cap City Poets* (Pudding House Publications), an anthology of central Ohio poets, and is currently editing an anthology for the Ohio Poetry Association.

Find Steve Abbot's work on pages 3-6

MJ Abell has published the chapbook *Below the Waterline* (Pudding House Publications) and received an Ohio Arts Council Fellowship. Her poetry performance, "Women Loving, Wild & Wise," celebrates the feminine through poetry, humor, and props displayed on an ironing board. She has created engaging workshops using marble hearts, fabric, and beads as sources for writing. She belongs to House of Toast Poets and WildSpirit Poetry Collective in Columbus.

Find MJ Abell's work on page 7

Nin Andrews is the author of five full-length collections of poetry and five chapbooks. Her next book, *Why God Is a Woman*, is due out from BOA in 2015.

Find Nin Andrews's work on pages 8-13

David Baker's many books include *Never-Ending Birds* (poems, Norton), and he was awarded the Theodore Roethke Memorial Poetry Prize in 2011. He has received fellowships and awards from the Guggenheim Foundation, NEA, Society of Midland Authors, Poetry Society of America, and Ohio Arts Council. A resident of Central Ohio since 1983, Baker teaches at Denison University and in the MFA program at Warren Wilson College. He is Poetry Editor of *The Kenyon Review*.

Find David Baker's work on page 14

Joshua Butts received his doctorate in English from the University of Cincinnati in 2009, and his M.A. from OSU. He teaches creative writing, literature, composition, and criticism at CCAD. He has published in various journals, including *Quarterly West*, *Harpur Palate*, and *Spinning Jenny*; his chapbook, *To Learn to Fingerpick Guitar*, was published by Pudding House Publications (2006). In 2012-13, Butts received a grant for a poetry project on Columbus native George Bellows.
Find Joshua Butts's work on pages 15-19

Nikkita Cohoon's poems have appeared in *Everyday Genius* and *elimae*, among others. Her artwork has appeared in *Dear Camera Magazine* and *Mid-American Review*. She is the online editor for *Black Ocean*.
Find Nikkita Cohoon's work on pages 20-27

Kevin Duffy is a recovering lawyer. He and his lovely wife Mary Ann are enjoying retirement in Columbus, with their three wonderful children and four grandchildren (and one on the way) living nearby.
Find Kevin Duffy's work on page 28

Sandra Feen teaches English and Creative Writing at Briggs High School, in Columbus. She holds an M.A. from Wright State University in Literature, and a B.F.A. in Creative Writing and B.S. in English Education from Bowling Green State University. Sandy is currently interpreting and performing work by Holocaust writers, in Susan Millard Schwarz's *Anahata Music Project.*
Find Sandra Feen's work on pages 29-30

Charlene Fix is a Professor of English at CCAD. She has received poetry fellowships from the Ohio Arts Council and the Greater Columbus Arts Council, and has published poems in various literary magazines (including *Poetry*, *Birmingham Poetry Review*, and *Rattle*). Her books include *Mischief* (Pudding House Publications), *Greatest Hits* (Katywompus Press), *Flowering Bruno* (XOXOX Press), *Harpo Marx as Trickster* (forthcoming from McFarland Publishers in 2013), and *Frankenstein's Flowers* (forthcoming from CW Books in 2014).
Find Charlene Fix's work on pages 31-34

Kate Fox's poems have appeared in *The Great River Review, New Virginia Review, Valparaiso Review, Mount Hope, West Branch,* and *Green Mountains Review,* among others. Her chapbook, *The Lazarus Method,* was published under the name of Kate Hancock by Kent State University Press as part of the Wick Poetry Chapbook Series. She earned her Ph.D. in American literature with an emphasis in creative writing from Ohio University. After serving for many years as the editor of the *Ohioana Quarterly* book review journal, she currently runs Textual Healing, a freelance writing and editing business.

Find Kate Fox's work on pages 35-37

Jennifer Hambrick's poetry has appeared in *Pudding Magazine, WestWard Quarterly, Common Threads,* and the *Ohio Poetry Day Best of 2011* prizewinners' collection, and is forthcoming in *A Narrow Fellow* and the 2013 Ohio Poetry Association anthology. Jennifer was a prizewinner in The Poetry Forum's 2011 William Redding Memorial Poetry Contest and the 2011 Ohio Poetry Day contests. By day, Jennifer Hambrick is a musician and public radio producer, broadcaster, and blogger.

Find Jennifer Hambrick's work on pages 38-39

Terry Hermsen teaches at Otterbein University, but previously spent twenty-five years doing poetry residencies in schools for the Ohio Arts Council. He has two chapbooks, *36 Spokes: The Bicycle Poems* and *Child Aloft in Ohio Theater,* from Bottom Dog Press. His book *The River's Daughter* was co-recipient of the Ohio Poet of the Year Award in 2009.

Find Terry Hermsen's work on pages 40-44

Krista Hilton has published poetry in *Cotton Boll/Atlanta Review, Number One, Mid-America Poetry Review,* and *Phase and Cycle.* Two poems were chosen by the Contemporary Gallery of the Kansas City Jewish Community Center for inclusion in an exhibit of visual art inspired by poetry. She currently teaches writing for Franklin University in Columbus, Ohio.

Find Krista Hilton's work on pages 45-46

Chad Jones is a poet and fiction author living and working in Central Ohio. He enjoys dogs and dislikes cancer.
Find Chad Jones's work on pages 47-48

Mark Sebastian Jordan works in the border region of Ohio's central highlands, one foot in rolling farmland, the other in rugged Appalachia. He is known as a playwright (*The Mansfield Trilogy*), a poet (*The Book of Jobs*), and a humorist (*1776 & All That, The News from Malabar*).
Find Mark Sebastian Jordan's work on page 49

Ariana-Sophia Kartsonis's first book, *Intaglio*, won the 2005 Wick Poetry Prize and was published by Kent State University Press. A collaborative chapbook, *By Some Miracle, a Year Lousy with Meteors*, won the Dreamhorse Press Chapbook Award and is forthcoming later this year. Her second full-length collection: *The Rub*, won the Elixir Press Editor's Prize and will be published in 2014. She is the faculty advisor for Botticelli Literary/Art Magazine of Columbus College of Art and Design.
Find Ariana-Sophia Kartsonis's work on pages 50-53

Matt Kilbane is from Cleveland, Rock 'n' Roll capital of the world. His work is forthcoming in the *2012 Best of the Net Anthology*. He serves currently as a Poetry Co-Editor for the *Sycamore Review*, and his favorite Ohio poet is Hart Crane.
Find Matt Kilbane's work on pages 54-59

Gail Martineau, a Denison University graduate, finds inspiration in the day-to-day lives of Central Ohioans. As a digital editor with 10TV News and previously as a journalist for the Dispatch companies, she has a unique vantage point from which to observe the struggle and triumphs of individuals in our community. Gail's creative writing is a reflection of those stories. Gail lives in Upper Arlington with her amazing partner Andrew and their six-year-old Sophie.
Find Gail Martineau's work on page 60

Alexis N. Misko is a new resident of Columbus, Ohio. She received a bachelor's degree in psychology with a minor in women's studies from Kent State University, and a clinical doctorate in occupational therapy from The University of Toledo. Alexis has always found solace in writing poetry, and hopes that her voice will continue to grow as she does.

Find Alexis Misko's work on page 61

Nathan Moore's work has appeared in various places including *Heavy Feather Review*, *Fleeting Magazine* and *Everyday Genius*. He is a co-organizer of the Columbus Poetry Forum in Columbus, Ohio.

Find Nathan Moore's work on pages 62-64

Brad Pauquette is a freelance writer and independent web developer in Columbus, Ohio. In 2010, he founded Columbus Creative Cooperative. His novelette *Sejal and the Walk for Water* is now available. Learn more at BradPauquette.com.

Find Brad Pauquette's work on pages 65-66

Cynthia Rosi emigrated from Seattle to London, England, at the age of 21, determined to write for a living. She worked in journalism, writing poetry and fiction on the side. At the turn of the millennium, Headline, UK published Cynthia's two mystery novels *Motherhunt* and *Butterfly Eyes* (now on e-book). In 2003, Cynthia moved with her husband to Columbus, Ohio. She spent time raising a family, and helped her husband start Via Vecchia Winery. Today she works full time as a freelancer, fiction writer, and commutes to Antioch's low-residency M.F.A. program in LA.

Find Cynthia Rosi's work on page 67

Alexis-Rueal is a Columbus, Ohio poet. She is a regular with the Writers' Block poetry group and was the first runner-up at the 2012 Columbus Arts Festival. Her first chapbook, *Letter to 20*, was released in 2013.

Find Alexis-Rueal's work on pages 40-44

Barbara Sabol is the author of two chapbooks, *Original Ruse* (Accents Publishing) and *The Distance Between Blues* (Finishing Line Press). Her poems have most recently appeared in *Bigger than They Appear: Anthology of Very Short Poems* (Accents Publishing, 2011), *The Louisville Review*, *Tupelo Press Poetry Project*, *The Examined Life* and *San Pedro River Review*. She holds an M.F.A. from Spalding University. Barbara is a speech therapist who lives and works in Cuyahoga Falls, OH.

Find Barbara Sabol's work on pages 70-74

Sherri B. Saines is a librarian at Ohio University, a good cover for various passions, such as poetry, 18th Century reenacting, and all kinds of dancing. She has been a writer since she was six years old, a confirmed poet by age twelve, and an academic by default. Her non-literary husband, Steve, is her best critic and greatest support.

Find Sherri B. Saines's work on pages 75-76

Jack Schwarz serves as both Spiritual Life Director and Chair of the Cultural Council at Twin Valley Behavioral Healthcare. Affiliated with several medical facilities, he provides an interfaith approach to pastoral care. Long ago, Jack taught writing and literature at two Ohio universities; subsequently, he toiled as a ghostwriter for the Ohio General Assembly. A former synagogue president and Jewish Community Chaplain for central Ohio, Jack also has enthusiastically supported animal protection groups and wildlife centers.

Find Jack Schwarz's work on pages 77-79

Natalie Shapero is the author of the poetry collection *No Object* (Saturnalia Books, 2013). Her poems have appeared in *The Believer*, *FENCE*, *The New Republic*, *Poetry*, and elsewhere. She lives in Gambier, OH, where she is a Kenyon Review Fellow.

Find Natalie Shapero's work on pages 80-83

Jordy Lawrence Stewart originates from the small town of Cedarville, Ohio. When he isn't busy writing or studying he also enjoys spending his time writing music, painting and diving into the various social scenes and creative landscapes of greater Columbus. He'd like to dedicate "Another Storm Poem" to his late grandfather.

Find Jordy Lawrence Stewart's work on pages 88-89

Joy Sullivan confessed to being a poet one night in a bar and a stranger's response was "We need poems like we need air." This is why she writes. It's just another way of breathing.

Find Joy Sullivan's work on pages 90-92

Dameion Wagner is a language arts teacher at a high school in Central Ohio. He finds it funny that when most people consider "language arts" they think "English," but they may not consider the art; Dameion never did until he began writing and teaching. He loves the writing, the reading, the revising... he loves trying to make the bones of his language into a good, solid stock.

Find Dameion Wagner's work on pages 93-94

Scott Woods is the author of *We Over Here Now* (2013, Brick Cave Books) and has published widely. He has been featured multiple times on National Public Radio. He was the President of Poetry Slam Inc. and MCs the Writers' Block Poetry Night in Columbus, Ohio. In April of 2006 he became the first poet to ever complete a 24-hour solo poetry reading, a feat he has bested every year since by performing without repeating a single poem.

Find Scott Woods's work on pages 95-100

About
Columbus Creative
Cooperative

Founded in 2010, Columbus Creative Cooperative is a group of writers and creative individuals who collaborate for self-improvement and collective publication.

Based in Columbus, Ohio, the group's mission is to promote the talent of local writers and artists, helping one another turn our efforts into mutually profitable enterprises.

The organization's first goal is to provide a network for honest peer feedback and collaboration for writers in the Central Ohio area. Writers of all skill levels and backgrounds are invited to attend the group's writers' workshops and other events. Writers can also find lots of resources and contructive feedback on our website.

The organization's second goal is to print the best work produced in the region.

The co-op relies on the support and participation of readers, writers and local businesses in order to function.

Columbus Creative Cooperative is not a non-profit organization, but in many cases, it functions as one. As best as possible, the proceeds from the printed anthologies are distributed directly to the writers and artists who produce the content.

For more information about Columbus Creative Cooperative, please visit **ColumbusCoop.org**.

About
Hannah Stephenson
Poetry Editor

Hannah Stephenson is a poet, editor, and instructor living in Columbus, Ohio. Her poems have appeared recently in *Huffington Post, Contrary, MAYDAY, qarrtsiluni,* and *The Nervous Breakdown*; her full-length collection, *In the Kettle, the Shriek*, is forthcoming from Gold Wake Press (October 2013).

She is the founder of Paging Columbus, a literary arts monthly event series with a local focus (held at The Ohio State University Urban Arts Space). To learn more about this series, visit pagingcolumbus.wordpress.com.

To read more of Hannah's work, you can visit her daily poetry site, The Storialist, at www.thestorialist.com.

Hannah Stephenson has graciously served as the editor for this poetry anthology, and Columbus Creative Cooperative is thankful for her efforts, initiative and the fantastic body of work that Hannah has produced.

Find Hannah's work on pages 84-87.

About
Yao Cheng
Artist

Yao has always loved to paint and draw. At an early age, her mother was her biggest supporter, taking her to art classes that introduced her to drawing and painting that captured her imagination. After her parents brought her to the United States from China years later, she carried her love for painting with her. After graduating from the Rhode Island School of Design in 2009 with a textiles degree, she went on to design print and pattern in the apparel industry for a few years before starting her own design studio.

Yao Cheng Design was founded in late 2012 in Columbus, Ohio. As the proud owner and designer, Yao combines her passion for painting with her love for surface patterns, producing textiles, desktop wallpapers and book covers. In addition, she sells archival art prints of her many favorite watercolor paintings on Etsy.

Yao's work is almost always in watercolor. She loves the lack of control, the way colors blend and the imprints her brush marks leave. Her painting is influenced by her study of Chinese calligraphy.

You can find more of her work on her website,
www.YaoChengDesign.com.

Yao Cheng provided the cover artwork for this anthology,
as well as the artwork on pages 2 and 101.

CPSIA information can be obtained at www.ICGtesting.com
Printed in the USA
BVOW071810030313

314555BV00001B/11/P